Table of Contents

Blueprint Publishing
5036 Dr. Phillips Blvd. Suite 124
Orlando, Florida 32819

The Blueprint for students to and through College
First Edition
2025 by Blueprint Publishing

ISBN: 978-09802391-3-3

Acknowledgments

First I would like to thank my lord and savior Jesus Christ for inspiring me to write this book. Second, I'll be honest; it is hard for me to write acknowledgments for the simple reason that my life as a father has been blessed with a multitude of parental influences. Of course, I have to begin with the love of my life Marquita. We've been together for some time now and have shared some great times together. To my children Desire and Destiny, you girls are growing up so fast, and I love you both dearly. To my mother I miss you dearly and I wish you could be here to enjoy this accomplishment. I love you always and I know you are watching over me.

Special thanks to my fraternity brothers the men of Phi Beta Sigma Fraternity, Inc. and Zeta Phi Beta Sorority, Inc.

To some of my mother's closest friends Lillie Thomas, Mildred Singleton, and Mary McCloud who are all excellent parents, thank you for being a positive and influential guide of what true parenting is all about.

The Thomas family, the McCloud, the Singleton family, the Rolle family, the Johnson family, the Lumpkin family, and the Decembert family.

If I didn't mention someone please don't take it personal, blame it on the head, and not the heart. Thank you to complex graphics for an awesome web site

<u>What to Do About Senioritis</u>

Seniors have worked hard for three years, taking tests, completing projects, and preparing for college admission. When senior year rolls around, some students just want to get through college applications and relax before they head off to the college of their choice.

Also known as senioritis, taking it easy senior year may seem like a nice break, but is likely to do more harm than good. According to recent reports, incomplete high school preparation can contribute to academic problems in college.

As many as half of all college students do not have adequate academic preparation, and are required to take remedial courses.

More than one quarter of the freshmen at four- year colleges and nearly half of those at two-year colleges do not even make it to their sophomore year.

Not only does senioritis jeopardize your chances for success later on in college, it can also affect your grades—and college admission officers pay close attention to your performance senior year.

Many students mistakenly believe that prepping for college ends after the eleventh grade. However, the senior year, the entire senior year, is actually of particular interest to colleges.

Many college applications require you to list your senior courses, including information about course levels and credit hours. It will be very obvious to the admission officers if you've decided to take the year off.

Many colleges also include as part of the application a form called the mid-year grade report. Your counselor completes this form with first-half grades and sends it to the colleges to which you've applied. It then becomes a crucial part of the application folder.

Many college acceptance letters include warnings to students such as "Your admission is contingent on your continued successful performance." This means colleges reserve the right to deny you admission should your senior year grades drop.

How to make the most of your Senior Year

Senior year is your opportunity to strengthen your skills and broaden your experiences, in school and out, to prepare for all of the challenges ahead. A successful senior year can help launch you on the path to a successful future.

You should take the most rigorous courses available, and be sure to continue taking college- track subjects. Consider AP® courses, which can also earn you credit at many colleges.

Your continued involvement in activities, sports, and volunteer work will help you stay active and focused throughout your final year. A great internship or career-focused job opportunity can help motivate you to start considering your career options. Meaningful and significant experiences will help prepare you to make informed decisions about your education and career goals.

If you're interested in pursuing a subject further, and have excelled at your high school classes so far, consider taking a class at a local college. This challenge can help you avoid sliding into an academic slump, and stimulate your interest in the possibilities of college.

Another option in many areas is middle college or early college high schools. These schools, normally located on community and four- year college campuses, allow students to spend their last two years taking classes in both college and high school. Early exposure to college classes introduces you to the rigor of college work while easing your transition from high school.

College Decision-Making Guide

If you've been accepted by more than one college, congratulations! Now you get to do the choosing. Here are some tips to help you make up your mind.

Do some soul-searching to figure out which of your colleges would provide the best fit for you. Which one offers the educational and social experiences you are seeking? Here is a list of factors you might want to think about:

Location: Urban, suburban, or rural campus? How far from home?

Size: How big is the student population? What about class size?

Mix of students: Is the college coed? Are there students from all over the country, with different backgrounds and experiences?

Academics: Does the college offer programs of study that interest you?

Extracurricular: Does the college have the types

and ranges of extracurricular activities you are interested in?

- Facilities: Will you have access to labs, computing centers, and music, theater, or athletic facilities?

Rank these characteristics in order of importance to you and see how well each college matches up.

Get Advice from People You Trust
Visiting a college's campus can help break a deadlock. It's up to you to choose the college you
want to attend. Although this decision is ultimately a personal one, it never hurts to ask for advice from people who know you well and care about your future.

- Talk to your parents: Find out how each school's costs will impact the family's finances. Be patient with your folks—picking a college can be an emotional process.

- Consult your advisors: Ask your teachers, coaches, mentors, and religious leaders about their college experiences. Find out what they liked best and least about their college years—you might gain a new perspective on what to expect of the next four years.

- Don't forget your counselor: Meet with your counselor. Your counselor knows you well and has years of experience helping students with college decisions.

Talk to Current Students

Get first-hand knowledge about what it's really like to attend a particular college from current students. Don't be afraid to ask frank questions— your future college will be home, school, and work to you for the next four years.

- Your counselor may be able to put you in touch with former high school students who are now attending your colleges.

- College admissions offices can also give you contact information for current students, advisors, and professors.

Visit Campuses

Visiting a college's campus can help break a deadlock if you can't decide between two or more colleges. At this point, a campus visit is less about facts and figures than intuition and whether or not you click with a school. Ask yourself, "Will I be happy on this campus? Can I really picture myself here?" Get a good feel for the school by talking to students, sitting in on a class, and eating in a dining
hall. Don't be afraid to trust your instincts.

Compare Your Financial Aid Awards

If you receive offers of financial aid from more than one college, use the College Board's tool to
compare:

- Total amount of aid awarded
- Family share of costs
- Percentage of gift aid (grants and scholarships) vs. self-help aid (work-study and loans) for up to four schools, side by side

Don't Rush Your Decision

Many colleges expect your final decision by May 1st, so you have about one month to make up your mind. It's understandable if you're tempted to make a snap decision, just to end the uncertainty and get the whole process over with. However, try to keep your options open in case circumstances change (e.g. your parents decide to appeal your financial aid package or you decide to change your intended major).

Decide and Reply

Once you've made a decision, send in your acceptance letter. Don't forget to inform all of the schools that offered you admission of your final choice. You're holding onto someone else's spot. A simple letter thanking them for their consideration, but declining their offer, will do.

Remember, there shouldn't be pressure to find the perfect college. Any number of schools can be good fits and make you happy.

<u>What if you're rejected: Now What?</u>

"We're sorry, but we won't be able to offer you a place in our first-year class. We had many qualified applicants this year...."

This is not how you wanted your college letter to read, but there it is. After all of the work you put into your application and the months of anticipation, it's understandable if you're upset about the outcome. However, it's important to keep rejection letters in perspective and to understand that you have options.

<u>Rejection Is Not Always About You</u>

Some students read rejection from a college as an indication that they don't have what it takes to succeed. However, admissions decisions are not a judgment from society. Colleges have many reasons for rejecting students, and there is always an aspect of randomness in the process.

Student merit is not the only factor in a school's decision. Schools also must address their own needs for a diverse population or for strength on sports teams or in specific degree programs. Neither you nor your parents should treat rejection as a personal failure.

What if you haven't gotten into any of the schools to which you applied? This can occur when if senior grades falter. This requires some reevaluation of your situation, but it's certainly not the end of the world. Here are some steps you can take:

- Talk to your counselor.

She has been through this before with other students and knows what to do.

Apply to schools whose deadlines haven't yet passed.

- Many colleges have late admissions policies or rolling admissions. Use college search to help you find schools that are still accepting applications.

- Apply to the same schools again. Some schools will reconsider your application if you take the SAT® again and improve your scores or if your grades shot up dramatically at the end of your senior year. Contact the admissions office.

- Ask for an explanation.

Was it your high school transcript? Your essay?

- Consider transferring to the college. If you spend a year at another school, you can prove to college admissions offices that you're motivated and ready for college-level work. Consider community college too.

Appealing Admissions Decisions

You can try to appeal your rejection, but most students don't win. Contact the admissions office for details on its appeal process. Some colleges will allow you to provide new academic information that could improve your chances of getting in, such as
updated grades. You may also be able to request a spot on its waiting list.

The Upside

There's an upside? Yes. Sometimes it actually helps to have a decision made for you. Maybe you had several colleges on your wish list, and wouldn't have had an easy time choosing just one. Plus, if you hadn't been turned down by at least one college, maybe you would always wonder if you should have set your sights higher.

Remember, there's no one perfect college. Any number of schools can be good fits and make you happy. Plus, you may not even realize how wonderful the college, curriculum, and your fellow classmates are until you're there—wherever "there" is.

Tips for Finding Your College Match

How can you find colleges that match your needs? First, identify your priorities. Next, carefully research the characteristics of a range of schools. Finally, match the two. Here are some college characteristics you should consider.

Size will affect many of your opportunities and experiences, including:

- Range of academic majors offered
- Extracurricular possibilities
- Amount of personal attention you'll receive
- Number of books in the library

When considering size, be very sure to look beyond the raw number of students attending. For example, perhaps you're considering a small department within a large school. Investigate not just the number of faculty members, but also how accessible they are to students.

Location

Do you want to visit home frequently, or do you see this as a time to experience a new part of the country? Perhaps you like an urban environment with access to museums, ethnic food, or major league ball games. Or maybe you hope for easy access to the outdoors or the serenity of a small town.

Academic Programs

If you know what you want to study, research reputations of academic departments by talking to people in the fields that interest you. If you're undecided, relax and pick an academically balanced institution that offers a range of majors and
programs. Most colleges offer counseling to help you find a focus.

In considering academic programs, look for special opportunities and pick a school that offers many possibilities.

Campus Life

Consider what your college life will be like beyond the classroom. Aim for a balance between academics, activities, and social life. Before choosing a college, learn the answers to these
questions:

- What extracurricular activities, athletics, and special interest groups are available?

- Does the community around the college offer interesting outlets for students?

- Are students welcomed by the community?

- Is there an ethnic or religious group in which to take part?

- How do fraternities and sororities influence campus life?

- Is housing guaranteed?

- How are dorms assigned?

Cost

Today's college price tag makes cost an important consideration for most students. At the

same time, virtually all colleges work to ensure that

academically qualified students from every economic circumstance can find financial aid that allows them to attend. considering cost, look beyond the price tag.

Diversity

Explore what you might gain from a diverse student body. Think about the geographic, ethnic, racial, and religious diversity of the students as a means of learning more about the world. Investigate
what kinds of student organizations, or other groups with ethnic or religious foundations, are active and visible on campus.

Retention and Graduation Rates
One of the best ways to measure a school's quality and the satisfaction of its students is to learn the percent of students who return after the first year and the percent of entering students who remain to graduate. Comparatively good retention and graduation rates are indicators that responsible academic, social, and financial support systems exist for most students.

.

Why Visit Colleges?

You hear it from colleges. Come visit! You hear it from your high school counselor. Have you visited any campuses yet? And you hear it from us. But what's the big deal about seeing a college?

A campus visit is your opportunity to get a firsthand view of a college. A college catalog, view book, or website can only show you so much. To really get a feel for the school, you need to walk around the quad, sit in on a class, and visit the dorms.

A visit also gives you the chance to talk to students, faculty, and financial aid and admissions folks. You can get answers to questions, such as:

What are the average class size, and the student to faculty ratio? Are most classes taught by professors or by teaching assistants?

- What is the campus meal plan like? How is the food?

- What is the make-up of the current freshman class? Is the campus fairly diverse?

- What's the social scene like? What kinds of activities are planned by the college's Residential Affairs?

- Is there ample space in dorms or does there seem to be a housing crunch?

- How many students are commuters/residents?

- Do I feel at home here? Is this what I pictured college to be?

Get Valuable Information

Pick up any official school material you see, such as brochures and financial aid forms. Don't forget to get business cards, too, so you'll have a real, live contact if you have a question about admissions or financial aid.

Student-produced material will give you a sense of what campus life is really like. Look around for newspapers and activity calendars. Check out bulletin boards, too, to see what bands are coming to the campus, parties are advertised, internships are posted, and generally what the day-to-day energy of the place is.

Is This College Right for You?

Ultimately, it's your decision. Listen to your gut. Do you feel comfortable walking around campus? Do you click with the students and faculty? Spending time on a campus allows you to determine if a school is a good match.

ps to Help You Survive and Thrive Your Freshman Year and Beyond

The first few weeks on campus are extremely critical for all new students. It is during this time that you make critical decisions that will have an effect on the rest of your life. Some of these 25 tips are critical during your first weeks, while the others are meant for longer-term guidance and survival. Whatever you do, be sure to be yourself and try to enjoy your college experience as much as possible. Expect to feel some stress and homesickness, but don't let these issues wear you down.

1. **Go to all orientations.** Do you really need to go on yet *another* campus tour? Yes. The faster you learn your way around campus -- and around all the red tape -- the more at ease you'll feel and the better prepared you'll be when issues arise.

2. **Get to know your roommate and others in your residence hall.** The people you live with, most of whom are going through similar experiences and emotions are your main safety net -- not only this year, but for all your years. You may change

roommates after the first semester or you may stay roommates for all four years -- just take the time to get to know your fellow first-year students.

3. **Get Organized.** In high school, the teachers tended to lead you through all the homework and due dates. In college, the professors post the assignments -- often for the entire semester -- and expect you to be prepared. Buy an organizer, a PDA, a big wall calendar -- whatever it takes for you to know when assignments are due.

4. **Find the ideal place for you to study.** It may be your dorm room or a cozy corner of the library, but find a place that works best for you to get your work done -- while avoiding as many distractions as possible.

5. **Go to class.** Obvious, right? Maybe, but sleeping in and skipping that 8 am class will be tempting at times. Avoid the temptation. Besides learning the material by attending classes, you'll also receive vital information from the professors about what to expect on tests, changes in due dates, etc.

6. **Become an expert on course requirements and due dates.** Professors spend hours and hours preparing course syllabi and calendars so that you will know exactly what is expected of you -- and when. One of the lamest excuses a student can give a professor: "I didn't know it was due today."

7. **Meet with your professors.** Speaking as a professor, I can assure you there are only upsides to getting to know your professors, especially if later in the semester you run into some snags. Professors schedule office hours for the sole purpose of meeting with students -- take advantage of that time.

8 **Get to know your academic adviser.** This is the person who will help you with course conflicts, adding or dropping courses, scheduling of classes for future semesters, deciding on majors and minors. This person is a key resource for you -- and should be the person you turn to with any academic issues or conflicts. And don't be afraid of requesting another adviser if you don't click with the one first assigned to

you.

9   **Seek a balance.** College life is a mixture of social and academic happenings. Don't tip the balance too far in either direction. One of my favorite former students always used to say her motto was to "study hard so she could play hard."

10   **Get involved on campus.** A big problem for a lot of new students is a combination of homesickness and a feeling of not quite belonging. A solution? Consider joining a select group -- and be careful not to go overboard -- of student organizations, clubs, sororities or fraternities, or sports teams. You'll make new friends, learn new skills, and feel more connected to your school.

11   **Strive for good grades.** Another obvious one here, right? Remember the words of the opening paragraph; while good grades could have come naturally to you in high school, you will have to earn

them in college -- and that means setting some goals for yourself and then making sure you work as hard as you can to achieve them.

12 Take advantage of the study resources on campus. Just about all colleges have learning labs and tutors available. If you're having some troubles, these resources are another tool available to you. Another idea: form study groups.

13 Make time for you. Be sure you set aside some time and activities that help you relax and take the stress out of your day or week. Whether its enlisting yoga techniques, watching your favorite television shows, or writing in a journal, be good to yourself.

14 Don't feel pressured to make a hasty decision about a career or a major. It doesn't matter if it seems as though everyone else seems to know what they're doing with their lives -- believe me, they don't -- college is the time for you to really discover who you are, what you enjoy doing, what you're good at, and what you want to be.

It's not a race; take your time and enjoy exploring your options.

15 Take responsibility for yourself and your actions. Don't look to place the blame on others for your mistakes; own up to them and move on. Being an adult means taking responsibility for everything that happens to you.

16 Make connections with students in your classes. One of my best students said his technique in the first week of classes was to meet at least one new person in each of his classes. It expanded his network of friends -- and was a crucial resource at times when he had to miss a class.

17 Find the Career Services Office. Regardless of whether you are entering college as undeclared or have your entire future mapped out, seek out the wonderful professionals in your college's career services office and get started on planning, preparing, and acting on your future.

18 Don't procrastinate; prioritize your life. It may have been easy in high school to wait until the last minute to complete an assignment and still get a good grade, but that kind of stuff will not work for you in college. Give yourself deadlines -- and stick to them.

19 Stay healthy/Eat Right. A lot of problems first-year students face can be traced back to an illness that kept them away from classes for an extended period of time that led to a downward spiraling effect. Get enough sleep, take your vitamins, and eat right. If you haven't heard the jokes about college food, you soon will. And without mom or dad there to serve you a balanced meal, you may be tempted to go for those extra fries or cookies. Stay healthy and avoid the dreaded extra "Freshman 15" pounds by sticking to a balanced diet.

20 Learn to cope with homesickness. It's only natural that there will be times when you miss your family, even if you were one of those kids who couldn't wait to get away. Find a way to deal with those f feelings, such as making a phone call or sending some email home.

21 Stay on campus as much as possible. Whether it's homesickness, a job, or a boyfriend or girlfriend from home, try not to leave campus too soon or too often. The more time you spend on getting to know the campus and your new friends, the more you'll feel at home at school. And why not take advantage of all the cultural and social events that happen on campus?

22 Seek professional help when you need it. Most colleges have health and counseling centers. If you're sick or feeling isolated or depressed, please take advantage of the many services these offices provide students. You don't have to face these issues by yourself.

23 Keep track of your money. If you've never had to create a budget, now is the time to do so. Find ways to stretch your money - and as best you can, avoid all those credit card solicitations you'll soon be receiving. The average credit card debt of college grads is staggering.

24 **Don't cut corners.** College is all about learning. If you procrastinate and cram, you may still do well on tests, but you'll learn very little. Even worse, don't cheat on term papers or tests.

25 **Be prepared to feel overwhelmed.** There's a lot going in your life right now. Expect to have moments where it seems a bit too much. As one student says, be prepared to feel completely unprepared. The trick is knowing that you're not the only one feeling that way.

Final Words of Advice

You've done all the prep work -- you've gotten good grades in high school, scored well on a standardized test, and been accepted into the college you want to attend -- so enjoy all your hard work while laying the groundwork for a successful college career. Don't be a statistic; be determined to make it through your freshman year -- and beyond. Take advantage of your network of new friends and professors, have fun while learning as much as you can, and get the most out of your college experience.

Reasons College Students Leave/Drop-Out

1. Too much fun at the expense of classes and grades

2. A sense of not belonging; a sense of isolation, homesickness

3. Academically unprepared; burned-out on education

4. Financial constraints; low on funds

5. Personal family issues

6. Academic climate/fit

7. Choice of wrong major; major not offered

8. Lack of advising, guidance

9. Demands from part-time or full-time employment

10. Move to a different geographic location

Time Management Tips for High School Students

Does it seem like there's never enough time in the day to get everything done? Feel like you're always running late? Here are some tips for taking control of your time and organizing your life.

1. Make a "To Do" List Every Day.

Put things that are most important at the top and do them first. If it's easier, use a planner to track all of your tasks. And don't forget to reward yourself for your accomplishments.

2. Use Spare Minutes Wisely.

Get some reading done on the bus ride home from school, for example, and you'll kill two birds with
one stone.

3. It's Okay to Say "No."

If your boss asks you to work on a Thursday night and you have a final exam the next morning, realize that it's okay to say no. Keep your short- and long-
term priorities in mind.

4. <u>Find the Right Time.</u>

You'll work more efficiently if you figure out when you do your best work. For example, if your brain handles math better in the afternoon, don't wait to do it until late at night.

5. <u>Review Your Notes Every Day.</u>

You'll reinforce what you've learned, so you need less time to study. You'll also be ready if your teacher calls on you or gives a pop quiz.

6. <u>Get a Good Night's Sleep.</u>

Running on empty makes the day seem longer and your tasks seem more difficult.

7. <u>Communicate Your Schedule to Others.</u>

If phone calls are proving to be a distraction, tell your friends that you take social calls from 7-8 p.m. It may sound silly, but it helps.

8. <u>Become a Taskmaster.</u>

Figure out how much free time you have each week. Give yourself a time budget and plan your activities accordingly.

9. <u>Don't Waste Time Agonizing.</u>

Have you ever wasted an entire evening by worrying about something that you're supposed to be doing? Was it worth it? Instead of agonizing and procrastinating, just do it.

10. <u>**Keep Things in Perspective.**</u>

Setting goals that are unrealistic sets you up for failure. While it's good to set high goals for yourself, be sure not to overdo it. Set goals that are difficult yet reachable. Consider these tips, but personalize your habits so that they suit you. If you set priorities that fit your lifestyle, you'll have a better chance of achieving your goals.

Surefire Tips for Succeeding in College

Take responsibility for your own learning. You're not in high school anymore. Everyone in college is there to learn because they want to, not just to pass because they have to. There are a lot of opportunities for learning in college, often times outside the classroom. Take advantage of every opportunity you can.

Appreciate your time in college. You'll never again have so many opportunities with so few responsibilities.

Take risks. College isn't just about getting good grades. It is a time to learn more about the world and yourself. Branch out and take risks Try something new. Meet new friends.

Expand your horizons. Classes do not have to only focus on your major or what is best for your future career. Try taking some elective classes in other subjects.

Set goals. Every term, reset your goals to keep you motivated and give you something to work toward.

Consider your personal interests when choosing your major. Don't just choose a major because of what the current job market is like or because it's what your friends or family members are doing. Choose a program that interests you and that you will enjoy studying.

Take some major courses as early as you can. If you can take a course within your major your freshman year, do so. You may learn that you want to switch majors. It's best to learn this as soon as you can.

Go abroad. Most colleges offer some type of study abroad program. You may be able to attend classes for a semester or year in Europe, Africa, Asia, Australia, or South America. Get to know the requirements for these programs early on so you can plan accordingly. Check out

Prepare for each class as though there would be a pop quiz. The benefit of this is two-fold: firstly, you'll be more able to participate in class; secondly, you'll be prepared if there actually is a pop quiz.

Read the syllabus for each of your courses. Understand how many exams there will be. Know how much each assignment is worth. Know what the professor expects of you.

Be on time for each class. Better yet, come early. Sit down and get relaxed before class begins. Professors like students who are always present and never late. Moreover, you'll be doing yourself a favor by knowing exactly what material was covered each day. If you have trouble actually getting up early and going to class, consider taking an online. More universities are beginning to make this an option.

Be attentive and stay focused. Avoid distractions such as instant messaging or crossword puzzles. Treat class as though it were an important business meeting. Your professor will appreciate it and you will learn more.

Ask questions. If the professor ever says something that you do not understand, never be afraid to ask for clarification. Chances are there are other students in class that also didn't understand.

Do not write down everything. Write in outline form so your notes will be easy to skim and review. Be sure to take clear, concise notes every class.

Use separate notebooks for each class. Or use subject dividers to separate your notes. Try to avoid taking notes for your psychology class in your math notebook. Doing so will make exam preparation much more difficult than it should to be.

Use a loose leaf notebook instead of a spiral bound notebook. Loose leaf notebooks are easier to organize, as they allow you to move your notes around or add handouts where necessary.

Try to make a friend in each class. If you have to miss a class, you can call your classmate and get the lowdown on what you may have missed. Also, often times partner projects are assigned and it is awkward to have to work with a stranger. If you already know someone in the class, it relieves any tension there may otherwise be.

Find a good place to study. Dorm rooms are often littered with distractions — television, video games, loud music, your roommate's girlfriend, etc. Find a quiet place that will work for you, whether it be a study lounge down the hall from your room or the library across campus. Treat studying like you're going to work each day.

Establish a routine study time. Getting into a rhythm at the beginning of every term will help you stay focused and disciplined. Lacking a routine may lead to bad habits or apathy.

Take breaks while studying. If you have several hours of studying to do the day before a big exam, break up your studying routine into 50-minute sessions, followed by five- or 10-minute breaks. Studying for several hours nonstop will not be very helpful.

Stay on top of your reading. Almost every college class will require reading. A lot of reading. Don't fall behind or it will cost you.

Prepare a list of questions to ask. As you're reading, you may come across some things that you don't fully understand. Write down these questions to ask your professor when you're in class the next day.

Use a highlighter. Highlight passages that are particularly important and that you should review further. Avoid highlighting entire pages.

Use a pencil. Write in the margins any notes you may want to make while you're reading. Then when you re-read the material a few weeks later for the final exam, you should just be able to go over these margin notes.

Use a dictionary. Improve your vocabulary by looking up any unfamiliar words you may come across as you're reading.

Find a study partner or two. Study partners can help you stay focused and can point out some things that you may have overlooked.

Get notes for any classes you may have missed. Never assume that you know what was covered in classes that you may have missed. Get notes from a classmate for that day.

Begin studying at least three days before an exam. Study for about two or three hours per day if you have to. But don't wait until the day before your exam to cram for eight hours. You won't remember much and you'll be worn out come test time.

Go to bed early the night before an exam. Getting plenty of rest the day before the exam will keep your mind sharp. You don't want to be feeling sleepy during an exam.

Arrive early on exam day. Take a seat five or 10 minutes before the exam starts to allow you time to relax and get your mind prepared for the challenge ahead.

Read the instructions of the test very carefully. You may know the material inside and out but that won't make one bit of difference if you can't obey simple instructions.

Review the entire test before you answer any questions. Plan ahead. If your exam period is 90 minutes long, don't spend an hour on the first part only to find out that there are still two equally challenging parts to go. Spend the first minute of the exam planning how much time you think you will need to spend on each question or section. Answer what you know first and then come back to more difficult questions.

Check the back of every page. Nothing feels worse than getting a test back and realizing you only answered half of the questions.

Be sure to answer the question in full. Read each essay question carefully, then read it again and again until you have a firm grasp on exactly how to answer it. You may have a terrific answer to give, but if you only answer half the question, that won't make for a very good grade.

Start early on those long term papers. Especially when a lot of research is involved, beginning the planning and outlining stages of a term paper weeks ahead of the due date will benefit you greatly. Be certain you can get all of the research materials you need before you begin writing.

Prepare an outline before you start writing. Never write a long paper from start to finish without taking a look at the big picture first. Outlining the entire paper before you begin will help you develop and convey your ideas better.

Use the writing center. Most colleges offer a writing center with assistants that will teach you how to become a better writer. Turn in your first drafts here and they will point out your writing flaws so you can improve. Often times, just one visit to the writing center could improve your paper a full letter grade.

Beware plagiarism. Taking credit for another person's thoughts or words by plagiarizing or cheating is grounds for expulsion at most colleges. Know how to cite your sources within your papers and do so consistently.

Don't believe everything you read on the Internet. The Internet is a powerful learning and research tool. While there are a lot of credible sources available online, be aware that anyone nowadays can set up a Web page. Just because it's online doesn't make it fact.

Seek counseling if you're lonely or depressed. Most college campuses offer a counseling center to offer aid to troubled students. Don't be afraid to take advantage of this resource if you need to.

Find a tutor if you need help. Your student peers or teaching assistants often serve as tutors in subjects that are giving you struggles. Seek them out and let them help you understand what the professor cannot. Often times, it's easier to learn from someone similar in age to you.

Take advantage of the library. It may not be as easy as doing a Google search, but the quality of the sources in a university library is second to none. You'll be able to research centuries-old articles from newspapers or read an entry from a scientific journal. Those are just two examples of things a university library can offer you that the World Wide Web cannot.

Find out who your advisor is and visit regularly, at least once per term. This will help keep you on track for graduation. Your advisor can also help you choose a major or give you recommendations on which classes you should take.

Get to know your professors. It is pretty easy to coast through college without ever getting to know your professors. It will take a bit of effort to get many of them to even learn your name. But doing so could really pay off when you need a letter of recommendation or if you plan on doing an independent study.

Know when your professors' office hours are. Try to visit each professor at least once per term. And never be afraid to go into office hours needing extra help or ask a question or two. Remember your professors are there to help you learn. Take advantage of that.

Get a suit. Wear it to any job interviews. Employers will expect you to dress your best when they first meet you.

Work on your resume. A resume isn't just another homework assignment that takes you 10 minutes to write up really quickly before class. This is a major document that will help you land a job after you graduate. Spend hours on it if you have to. Seek help from a career counselor so you know what you should include and how it should be formatted.

Visit the career center. The guidance counselors are there to help you work on your resume and job interviewing skills. They want to help you. So let them. Schedule appointments and try to attend their sessions at least once each term. Don't be afraid to see a career counselor even if you're just a freshman. It's never too early to start planning your future.

Go to career fairs. Most college campuses will have at least one career fair per year. Attend it. You'll get a chance to mingle with potential employers and find out what careers are available to you after college.

Find a summer internship. Don't blow your summer sitting on the couch in your parents' house. Do something for your future by securing an internship. You may not get paid much, if anything, but you are very likely to help land yourself a job after graduation.

Be on time for job interviews. In your junior and senior years, you may have the opportunity to interview with potential employers. This is your first impression on them. Make it a good one.

Consider every possible source of financial aid. Check with your school's financial aid and admissions offices, your academic college, your church, clubs or special interest groups to which you or your parents belong, professionals working in your major field, scholarship resource books, and honor societies and fraternities.

Don't give up on your financial aid **search.** You may not find a lot of education money right away. But stick with it because you could save thousands of dollars.

Know the guidelines and due dates of paperwork for your financial aid awards. And be sure to stay on top of this. Nothing could be worse than losing a scholarship or financial aid award because you lost some paperwork or missed a due date. A mistake like this could cost you thousands of dollars.

Never buy new textbooks... unless you enjoy improving your college bookstore's bottom line. Buying new textbooks is for suckers and can put a huge hole in your budget. Always try to buy a used textbook or even check out a copy from your library before you buy a new textbook. You could save a couple hundred bucks each term.

Shop early for books. You'll find the best selection of used materials. If you don't get to the bookstore until a week or two into the new term, chances are they'll be out of used materials by then and you might be stuck having to purchase a new textbook at an outrageous price.

A credit card is not free money... no matter how often you are bombarded with advertisements that may lead you to believe otherwise. If you do get a credit card, just be sure to pay off the amount in full each month, or you will start to get into deep credit card debt. Deep debt can prevent you from getting a car or a house mortgage later in life. On the positive side, paying your credit card bills in full on time will help establish your personal credit.

Set a budget. And stick to it. Figure out how much money you make each month and estimate how much you will spend each month. Never spend more than you earn.

Don't blow all your money. Most college students are on a tight budget. Don't blow all of your money on alcohol or junk food. Put a little into a savings account each month, even if it's not that much.

Get a part-time job to make some extra cash. If you live on campus, an on-campus job in food services, with a professor, or in one of the college offices might be worth looking into. At some schools, tutoring or working for the school newspaper will pay you, too.

Use your meal plan. It'll save you a lot of money to eat what you've already paid for. Also, your dining hall will usually be much healthier than eating from the dollar menu at a fast food restaurant.

Watch those cell phone minutes. Running up your cell phone bill is very easy to do, as cell phone service providers charge huge premiums for each minute of overuse. Most plans allow for free nights and weekend minutes. So if you have a call to make that can wait until then, it could save you big bucks.

Know off-campus costs. If you want to move off campus, be aware of the additional costs of living.

Don't procrastinate. Whatever the assignment may be, if you have some free time, just do it now. Otherwise, you'll be stuck doing it later. If an assignment takes longer than you had expected, you'll have wished that you had begun it sooner instead of waiting until the last minute.

Use a planner or calendar to keep track of due dates. Missing a paper deadline or forgetting exam dates is inexcusable. Avoid this by shelling out a few bucks for a planner. And use it regularly.

Set priorities and don't be afraid to cut back on a few things. Being captain of the lacrosse team, student government president, and editor of the yearbook all while getting a degree in chemical engineering might look great on a resume, but for most people, taking on so many activities is impractical. Take a serious look at what is important to you. If you feel overloaded, don't be afraid to drop an activity or two.

Time is on your side. There are 168 hours in each week. If you set aside 56 hours for sleep and 40 hours for academics, that leaves you with 72 hours for everything else.

Leave reminders for yourself. Have a meeting tomorrow at noon? Leave a post-it note on your door so you don't forget.

Avoid time wasters. As fun as it may be to stay up all night watching television or playing John Madden, perhaps you shouldn't do so with a big paper due the next day.

When living in the dorm, take it all in stride. You may be required to live in a dorm your freshman year. Don't expect much in terms of privacy, personal space, quiet time, or even cleanliness. But enjoy some of its perks, namely the camaraderie with your dorm mates and the proximity to your classes.

Avoid athlete's foot. Invest in a pair of shower shoes, especially if you live in a dorm with a communal shower.

Lock your doors. You may have a lot of valuables in your room — computer, jewelry, clothes, stereo, television. Don't make it easy for someone to come in and take something.

Party. Mingle and meet people. Don't stay locked up in your room or your library all the time. Go out and enjoy yourself every once in a while. Just don't party too hard too frequently.

Join a student organization. Whether it be student government or ballroom dancing, join a club of other people with similar interests to your own. You'll make close friends and do activities that you enjoy.

Join an intramural team. Not only will this help you stay in shape, but you'll make new friends with your teammates.

Join a club in your major. Most majors will have some sort of honors society or extracurricular club on campus. Joining such a club will get you involved with other students in your classes and will likely put you in personal contact with one or two of the professors, as they are often the moderators of these clubs.

Eat healthy. Your mom's home cooked meals are no longer an option. Try to eat at your dining hall as often as you can and be sure to eat your fruits and vegetables. A diet of greasy pizza and beers every night isn't exactly first-rate eating.

Exercise. P.E. classes usually are not required in college as they were in high school. Account for this by going on runs, using the student gym, or simply throwing the football around.

Find out what health services has to offer. Many university health service centers offer free flu shots, STD testing, and birth control.

Take care of yourself when you're sick. You mom is no longer around to make sure you get plenty of fluids and chicken noodle soup. You'll have to do

this on your own. Check out Web MD's If you're sick for more than a day or two, consider seeing a doctor or nurse at the university health center.

Get plenty of rest. Seldom do college students get enough sleep. Try to get as much sleep as you can each night. Doctors recommend at least eight hours per night for college aged students.

Be safe. Get the scoop on underage drinking, drugs, and sex. If you're ever uncomfortable, just say no.

Designate a driver or have enough cash for a cab. Never take a ride home from a drunk friend. It's a good way to get killed. Take a cab if you need to. A few extra bucks spent could save your life.

Be lawful. Getting into trouble with the law could cause your scholarships to be revoked or could even get you expelled from school. Also be sure to read the campus rule book for any special university rules you may be expected to follow.

Pack lots of underwear and socks. You don't really need to do laundry until you run out of these two essentials.

Homesickness is natural. Almost every freshman experiences it. Just know that you're not alone and that you will get over it.

Become familiar with your college town. Know where the local grocery store, gas station, pharmacy, and hospital are. You may need them all at some point during your college career.

Make travel plans well in advance. Are you planning to fly home for Thanksgiving or Christmas? Want to take a trip to Aruba for spring break? Make sure to start planning well in advance. You'll get the best rates on flights if you start looking at least two months ahead of time. Considering all of the learning experiences in front of you, college should be the best years of your life. Appreciate the time you have as a college student. There are a lot of opportunities for you in a time when you will have relatively few responsibilities. Of course, everyone will undergo struggles in this
period, but that is part of what makes college so unique and challenging. Don't be afraid to take advantage of the resources at your fingertips while you have them there. Seize the day, and remember, as Tom Petty once said, "The work never ends, but the college does."

<u>College Survival Tips</u>

The jump to college can be stressful. You're leaving behind your school, friends, family, and home, and
going off to explore a new place, make new friends, learn new things, and set your own priorities.

Many students overlook the stress involved in making so many big changes in such a brief period of time. The more prepared you are for college when you get there, the more ready you'll be to confront any new pressures. Here are some realities to consider, and a few common-sense ways to help you handle them:

Courses are at a higher level than high-school classes and the material is presented at a faster pace. Plus, professors are likely to assign more reading, writing, and problem sets than you may be used to.

All first-year college students contend with this bend in the learning curve, so don't think having to struggle to keep up is somehow a failing on your part. Give yourself an opportunity to adjust gradually to the new academic demands.

Choose a course load that includes some challenging classes and others that will be less intense.

You are responsible for managing your time in college. If you cut classes and don't do assignments, no one will nag you. You may wish they had if it comes time for the final and you don't know the material.

Buy a calendar and make sure you write down when and where your classes meet, when assignments are due, and when tests will take place. Give yourself ample time to study rather than waiting until the last minute and pulling an all- nighter.

You may not have the same day-to-day support system as you do now. For example, how will you manage your money and debt, especially when credit card companies are bombarding you with offers? Who is around to make sure you're not getting sick or run down? Factors like stress, late- night parties, and generally pushing yourself too hard can take a toll.

Don't always do what's easiest at the time. Make smart decisions. For example, when it

comes to your money, stick to a budget and use credit cards wisely. When it comes to your health, get enough sleep, eat well, and pay attention to what your body tells you. You'll need energy to enjoy all that college has to offer.
New social opportunities (and pressures) abound. Suddenly, you can recreate yourself in any way you want.

While forming new friendships can be exhilarating, true friendships are formed slowly, and the beginning of college can consequently be a lonely time. If you're unsure about participating in certain social scenes or activities, don't hesitate to seek guidance about the best ways to resist these pressures. Talk to parents, trusted friends from high school, and college counselors.

College is full of resources—professors, tutors, counselors, and often resident advisors. In college, it is up to you to initiate getting help. The good news is that once you do adjust to college life, it opens new doors to all sorts of learning—and living.

Flash forward to your first week at college...

College Roommate Rules

10:00 p.m.: You've finished your schoolwork for the evening. You neatly stack your books on your desk, fold and put away clothing, shut off the lights, slip into your neatly made bed, and drift off to sleep.

11:30 p.m.: You're jolted out of your peaceful dream by loud heavy metal and bright lights. Could it be morning already? No such luck. Rather, it seems your party-loving roommate has just arrived home from—surprise, surprise—a party (for the sixth night in a row) and is just now starting her homework. You watch in amazement (and frustration) as she simultaneously powers up her computer, dances to the music filling your small room, and discards her clothes and books on the floor. "Hey!" she yells over the music, noticing you for the first time. "What's up?" she asks, seemingly unaware that you were fast asleep.
You flop back onto your bed, put your pillow over your head and groan. "How am I ever going to get through the year?" you wonder.
Scenes like this are not unusual. Getting along with a roommate is a real concern, and one you

may be facing for the first time. If you're a bookworm who goes to bed early and your roomie is a party animal who just gets going at midnight, sharing the same quarters may not be easy. But that doesn't mean the two of you can't get along.

Perhaps the most important lessons you'll learn in college are the ones you learn outside the classroom. Figuring out how to live with someone involves respecting differences, sharing, being courteous, accepting others for who they are, and much more. You'll find that sharing space builds character.

While most freshmen do miss the privacy of their homes, they also find comfort in sharing company with others who are experiencing the same issues—difficult courses, living away from home, balancing school work and social life, and a whole lot more. In fact, while there are many alternatives for roommates who don't get along, most do stick it out, and solve their problems by talking it out.

Keeping lines of communication open is essential. Before you even step foot in your dorm, give your roommate a call and find out who you'll be living with for the next year. Here are some tips for getting off to a good start:

Discuss important issues and establish rules. If you can't study with music on, then come to an agreement about quiet hours. If she likes to have lots of friends in the room all the time, and you don't, make a schedule so that you can both enjoy the room at different times. If your roommate would rather you didn't study with the light on when she's trying to sleep, she should tell you. If you make house rules, and communicate openly and often, you can avoid unpleasant surprises down the road.

Be respectful. Successful roommate relationships are based on mutual respect. If your roommate doesn't like anyone borrowing her clothes, respect her wishes. If you don't like music on while you're studying, she should respect your needs, too.

Be willing to compromise. You and your roommate may not agree on everything, but you both have to be willing to compromise a little bit. If you're a slob and she's a neat freak, you should start cleaning up, at least in the parts of the room you share. And she should try to be flexible and realize your unmade bed doesn't affect her.

Be courteous. Courtesy is contagious. If you behave politely to your roommate, she will likely follow your lead. Take messages when people call for her. Wish her luck on an exam. Ask if you can pick up something for her while you're running errands. And, don't borrow anything without asking. Good friendships often begin by sharing space with strangers. So, who knows... maybe that loud, partying roommate you thought you'd never last with will become your good friend.

The Power of Study Groups

Have you ever noticed that when you explain something you've learned in class to a friend, you begin to understand it better yourself? This happens because when you explain, or teach, an idea, you need to actively think it through. And by thinking more deeply about what you've learned and then explaining it to someone else, you begin to understand it better. Studying with others in a small group is helpful to everyone because, as in the example above, you

- Think out loud.
- Share ideas.
- Learn from one another.

As the old saying goes, "Two heads are better than one." While studying alone may work well for things such as memorizing facts, sometimes you'll need to understand complicated ideas. And rather than memorize facts, you'll be required to apply facts to solving problems. Effective study groups involve hashing out lesson materials together—explaining concepts, arguing about them, figuring out why one person's answer differs from another's—and in the process, you learn more than you ever would have studying by yourself.

The Benefits of Study Groups

Group study offers other advantages, in addition to gaining a deeper understanding of class material. These include the following:

Took horrible notes in AP® French last week? No worries! A member of your study group can share his.

Each person brings different strengths to a study group, such as organizational skills, the ability to stick to a task, a talent for memorization, and so on.

Three study group members may be able to solve a calculus problem that none would have solved alone.

Members of a study group often have common goals, such as good grades. The work each person in a group does affects the other members, which results in making the group members supportive of one another.

It's more fun to study with others. And because it's more fun, you spend more time studying!

Guidelines for Getting a Group Together

How do you put a study group together? How many members should the group have? For how long should you meet? For answers to these questions and more, check out the following study group guidelines:

Create a group of four to six people. In a larger group, it's easy for someone to get left out, and smaller groups can too easily get off track.

Pick classmates who seem to share your interest in doing well in class. Look for people who stay alert in class, take notes, ask questions, and respond to the teacher's questions. John Mitchell, who has researched group work at Central Michigan University, suggests including in your study group "someone who understands the material better than you and someone who understands less." Doing so will provide you with someone who can explain concepts to you and someone to whom you can explain the material.

Hold study group sessions in a place that is free of distractions and that has room to spread out books, and notes.

Study groups should meet for no more than two to three hours at a time. Having a time limit will help the group focus. If you know you only have an hour, you're more likely to stay on task.
If possible, try to meet on the same day and time each week. Treating the study session as you would other activities helps you to keep to a schedule and ensures that everyone will attend.

Getting the Most Out of a Study Group Session

The greatest benefit of studying with a group of classmates is the support you receive from one another. Here are some tips to help your group get the most out of each study session:

Knowing what you want to achieve at each session helps the group stay focused and manage time. At the start of each meeting, a designated session leader should state what the goals are. For example, the session leader might announce, "Today we'll review chapter 7 and discuss the theorems introduced in class on Wednesday."

Before a session, be sure to finish your assigned reading, review notes, and list topics you want to go over. By being well prepared, your group can make the most of your time together by questioning one another on the assigned material.

When you instruct the group, you not only help the other group members, but also reinforce your own knowledge.

For each session, assign one member to be the taskmaster. This person's job is to steer the group members back to the topic if they begin to drift. Also, schedule five-minute breaks into your study sessions after every half hour or so of work. This allows all the group members to get off-topic chatting out of their systems.

By supplementing your individual study with a study group, you can reinforce what you've learned, deepen your understanding of complex concepts, and maybe even make a few new friends. Whoever said learning can't be fun?

First day tips for the Work World

The first day you pack a briefcase and head off to a professional job interview may seem far away, but the time to build strong skills and valuable habits is now. School is full of opportunities to develop the qualities most important to employers.

10 Key Qualities

1. Writing Skills

If you dread essays and other writing assignments,
consider this: in a recent survey of employers, communication topped the list of skills they look for most. By doing your best on every research paper
and lab report you write, you're preparing yourself for a career.
Health professionals keep patient charts, researchers and artists depend on the money they collect by writing grant applications, software engineers write technical specifications, and nearly everyone writes email to people inside and outside their organization. And before you even get the chance to interview, you'll need to represent yourself in cover letters and résumés.

2. Speaking Skills

Next time you're assigned a class presentation, think twice before dismissing it as an unimportant part of your education. Employers look for speaking skills in job hopefuls and it's never too soon to practice good eye contact and other public speaking techniques.

3. Teamwork Skills

How many times a week does your class count off and break into small groups to tackle a challenge? You practice voicing your opinions, listening and responding to others, and reaching compromises.

By the time you leave high school, you can be an expert in teamwork, an increasingly important skill in today's workplace.

4. Problem-Solving Skills

Problem solving goes far beyond your algebra textbook. Every school assignment is an opportunity to weigh all possible solutions carefully and select the one you think is best. As a working professional, you'll keep solving problems, whether computer programming bugs or budget shortfalls.

5. Initiative

Every time you raise your hand in class, every time you choose your own research topic, every time you interpret a piece of literature, you take initiative. And employers value can-do professionals who come up with new ideas and chart their own course through
projects.

6. Cool Under Pressure

Who hasn't made the argument that testing isn't a real-life situation? It's not like your future boss is
going to ask you to translate a Spanish passage without a dictionary in under 20 minutes. But try thinking of the pressure of testing as practice for the work world's own explosive situations. You could someday find yourself meeting tight deadlines, speaking with irate customers, holding a scalpel, or
handling dangerous chemicals.

7. Attention to Detail

When you double-check your calculations for a math problem, make sure you're using the correct homonym in an essay, or cite sources carefully in a
research paper, you're paying close attention to detail. That habit will come in handy in any workplace, whether you maintain a database,

keep a log of the hours you spend with clients, or simply write emails.

8. Time Management

How many classes do you attend each day? How many homework assignments do you tackle each night? And what about sports practice, play rehearsal, and other extracurricular? You have the chance to be a real pro when it comes to juggling the many demands on your time—and that's a good thing since most jobs require multitasking. Examples of on-the-job juggling feats include taking care of current clients while attracting new ones, responding to emails while working on a major presentation, and ordering tomorrow's produce while planning next week's menu.

9. Honesty

Employers need to know that they can trust you with everything from credit cards to trade secrets. But
how can you work at honesty? Every day that you do your own homework and resist the temptation to cheat on exams, you exercise your integrity muscle.

10. Love of Learning

Last but not least, a love of learning will see you through the initial weeks of a new job. It will also serve you well as you advance in your working life, taking on new projects, building expertise, and branching into new areas of interest. While your grandparents may have worked for the same company their entire lives, today's workforce is mobile, with most people changing careers, not just jobs, throughout their lifetime.

Resume Writing 101

Before you rush out to find that perfect job or internship, you'll need to write your resume. And not just any resume, but the kind that'll separate you from all the people applying to your college of choice or eager to land that dream job. Here are some ways to avoid the pitfalls of resume writing and land yourself in the spot light.

Lisa was just weeks away from finishing her junior year in high school and still looking for a summer internship. She always wanted to be a nurse, so she sent her resume to several local hospital recruiters, but was just not getting any responses.

Panicked and sure she'd be jobless for the summer, Lisa passed her resume to her family for constructive criticism. They all told her the same thing: her resume did not reflect enough experience and education related to nursing. She did include her volunteer work at the neighborhood health clinic, but she mostly listed jobs as a cashier and her involvement with school sports.

A lot of students think a generalized resume describing everything they've ever done is a great way to get any kind of job or internship. Not true. The first rule of thumb for resume-writing is to only include information that is useful to the job you're applying for. For example, Lisa's experience as a cashier would have come in handy if she was applying for a job in retail or sales.

If you're applying for summer jobs or internships in a variety of fields, be prepared to write more than one resume. Once you have the first done, use it as a template and just cut and paste the most relevant information for different jobs.

\

The Four Key Elements of a Resume'

Four main themes you should always include on your resume, no matter where you're applying, are volunteerism, association memberships, computer proficiency, and knowledge of other languages.

1. Volunteerism

No matter where you're applying or what you plan to study in college, potential employers want to know you're a well-rounded member of society. Listing your participation in volunteer work is important.

2. Association Memberships

It's also an added bonus for younger high school students to list any associations they've belonged to, such as:

- National Honor Society (N.H.S.)

- National Art Honor Society (N.A.H.S.)

Juniors and seniors probably have more experience in this area, but never underestimate participation in group roles. This includes any other club participation at school or in your community.

3. # Computer Proficiency

Let's face it, technology is everywhere. Knowledge of computers will most likely be a requirement for

just about any job. List any and all experience you have with computers, naming the actual program names you're familiar with (Word, Excel, PowerPoint, and Photoshop).

4. # Other Languages

The world is getting smaller and smaller, especially in the job market. Knowing a second or third language can put you at an advantage in qualifying
for a job and will certainly separate you from other candidates.

Putting It All Together

While you definitely shouldn't go over a page, don't feel that you have to use the resume template that's

found in most word processing programs. These models, though helpful, are often generic-looking. It's good to go the extra mile and show employers that you are as creative as you are intelligent. Differences in formatting (bullets, borderlines, or headings), fonts, styles, and sizes will catch the eye
and draw attention to the most important information.

Organization

You can organize your resume in many different ways, but the following order is one of the most common. Use it to help you get started.

Objective: state what kind of job or internship you're looking for.

Experience: describe your job history.

Education: just list your high school, unless you've taken college courses on the side.

Other Skills/Information: this is where you list your computer or language skills and any associations or memberships to which you've belonged.

Action Words

Be sure to describe your roles and accomplishments with strong action words and key
terms that will pop out at employers, usually ones that signify leadership and team roles you've had. These include words such as: team work, team player, multi-tasking, executed, organized, performed, maintained, supervised, managed, directed, developed, implemented.

Writing Style

The wording of your resume is just as important as the look. You may have to write several rough drafts to come up with one that will really shine. Here are a few writing style rules to keep in mind:

- Use matching verb tenses.

- Keep all descriptions short. Descriptions should generally take up no more than three to four lines on the page.

- Full sentences are not necessary, but be consistent with punctuation.

Resume Resources

Several job search engines have resume-building pages on their websites that will give you step-by- step guidelines to writing a resume. Some popular sites to check out include:

- Monster Jobs, www.monster.com

- CareerBuilder, www.careerbuilder.com

- MSN Careers, www.careers.msn.com

While these sites are free, they also offer resume- writing services you can order for a fee. It's always best to learn on your own, however, because knowing how to write a resume properly is a valuable skill you'll have for a lifetime.

The Final Word

I would like to congratulate you on working hard and achieving educational greatness. In this present day becoming a senior in high school and entering college isn't a guarantee.

I have listed many encouraging tips and advise that will help you if you use it. We at Blueprint Publishing can only give you the tools to succeed and it is up to you to use these tools illustrated in this book.

I am truly proud of all young adults that pursue their dreams through education or entrepreneurship. Good luck to you in all of your endeavors.

Dr. Donovan D. Davis

THE BLUEPRINT OF A SUCCESSFUL CLASSROOM
WHAT IT TAKES TO DISCIPLINE CHILDREN IN A CLASSROOM
The BLUEPRINT Of A Successful Classroom
WHAT IT TAKES TO DISCIPLINE CHILDREN IN A CLASSROOM
Donovan D. Davis
PRICE: $24.95
Tel: 1-888-264-6168
www.askdonovandavis.com

THE BLUEPRINT
TO AND THROUGH
COLLEGE
A RESOURCE GUIDE FOR
HIGH SCHOOL SENIORS AND
COLLEGE FRESHMEN
The BLUEPRINT
to and
through College
A RESOURCE GUIDE FOR HIGH SCHOOL SENIORS & COLLEGE FRESHMEN
Donovan D. Davis
PRICE: $14.95
Tel: 1-888-264-6168
www.askdonovandavis.com

THE BLUEPRINT
OF PARENTING
BRIDGING THE GAP BETWEEN
US AND OUR CHILDREN
The
BLUEPRINT
Of Parenting
BRIDGING THE GAP BETWEEN US AND OUR CHILDREN
Dr. Donovan D. Davis
PRICE: $14.95
Tel: 1-888-264-6168
www.askdonovandavis.com

THE BLUEPRINT
OF RECOVERY
STORIES OF ADDICTS AND THERE
JOURNEY THROUGH ADDICTION
The
BLUEPRINT
Of Recovery
STORIES OF ADDICTS AND THERE JOURNEY THROUGH ADDICTION
Donovan D. Davis
Certified Addictions Counselor
PRICE: $14.95
Tel: 1-888-264-6168
www.askdonovandavis.com

www.ingramcontent.com/pod-product-compliance
Lightning Source LLC
Chambersburg PA
CBHW031325060726
47590CB00003B/1331